INTRODUCTION

Have you ever caught yourself saying, "Oh, I'm so stupid," or "Dang! I always do this wrong." These lighthearted comments do more damage than we perceive. Labelling ourselves as 'stupid' or 'careless' may seem harmless at the beginning. But labels stick - first in our minds and then in others'. Soon enough, any mistake on your part would be attributed to that label.

For some of us, it takes a lifetime to prove these labels wrong. In the process, we go through discouragement and even depression.

Quite often, we use self-deprecation as a way to appear modest. In our attempt to uplift others, we tend to belittle ourselves. These offhand comments go into the core of our being and gradually change our perception of ourselves. It affects our self-esteem negatively. This, in turn, impacts our behaviour, relationships and state of mind.

What if the process were reversed? If you exchanged self deprecating insults for powerful, affirmative proclamations, what impact would that have on your being?

- So you made a mistake. Wonderful! Now you can learn more.
- So you piled on a few pounds. That's alright. You are human.
- So you lost your cool at work. Isn't it better to be passionate than detached?

It's time that we tell that internal, mean voice that constantly puts us down, to get lost. It seems easier said than done, but self care affirmations are an amazing first step to regain your confidence and promote inner healing.

Your mind believes what you tell it. It trusts you and your words. It responds to your voice and as you repeatedly affirm love and encouragement, it positively shapes thoughts, actions and ultimately, your future.

Self love affirmations proclaim the deep yearnings of your spirit. These daily sayings promote confidence, love and self esteem. Repeat them daily. Believe in them. Connect the words with your mind and heart. Say what you believe and believe what you say.

I AM
Enough

I attract
ABUNDANCE

I

ACKNOWLEDGE

---

all of me

I am my
healer

I am

KIND

NATURE *loves* ME BACK

I am

UNAPOLOGETICALLY

myself

I am
SAFE
in my
body

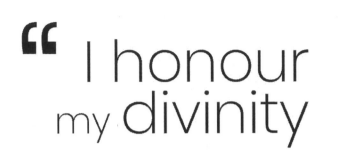

" I honour my divinity

I AM
Smart

I let
GO
and I let
GOD

I *am*
BRAVE

I am *light*

I am
∶STRONG∶

MY HEART IS MY
HOME

I am
proud of
myself

I honor my
commitments
to myself

I make a

DIFFERENCE

I cannot be

REPL
ACE
D

I *love* the
person *I am*
becoming

I meditate

I
respect
myself

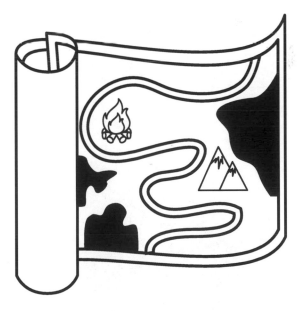

I master
[self-love]

I TRUST MY

feelings

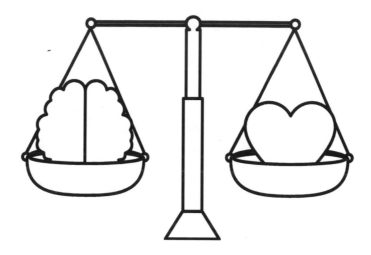

I *trust*
my *intuition*

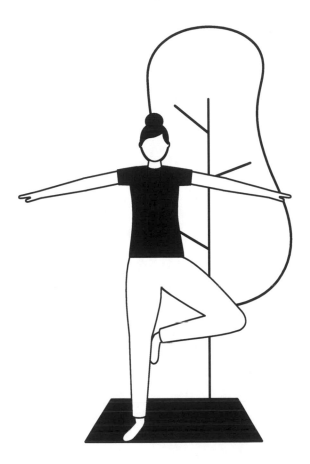

I trust
my body

I LISTEN
TO MY
body

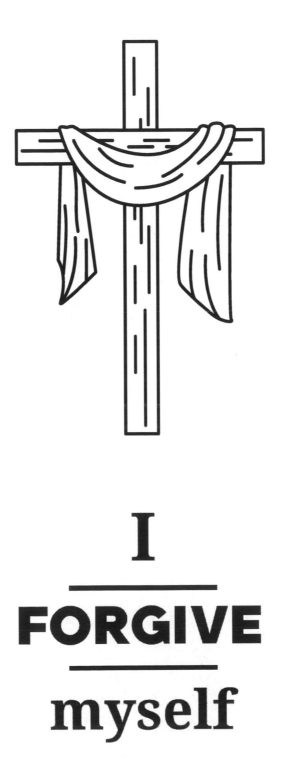

I
___

FORGIVE
___

myself

I *appreciate* me

I AM EVERYONE *pushed out*

I AM DEEPLY
LOVABLE

[just the way I am]

I *matter*

I reveal my

TRUE SELF

I AM *deeply*
SIGNIFICANT

I am _here_
for a reason

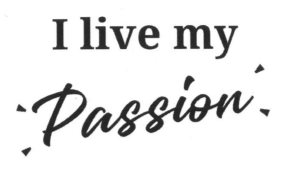

I live my
Passion

I am the
- *Creator* -
of my reality

I am **FREE** of worry

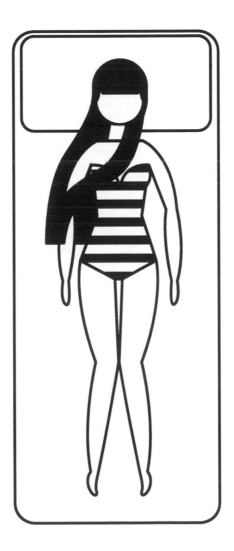

I choose to be
Positive

I *choose*
to love

I CHOOSE TO CREATE
ABUNDANCE

I AM NOT MY MISTAKES

Mistakes are *my* lessons

I am
HERE

ALL I NEED IS
[already]
WITHIN ME

I AM IN CHARGE
OF HOW I
feel today

I love [ALL]
of me

I deserve
the **BEST**

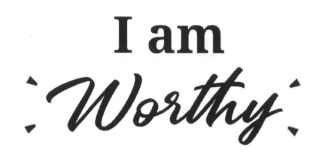

I am Worthy

I BREATHE
in confidence

I easily accept love that surrounds *me*

I have a [mission]

I COMMAND
my emotions

I am
filled and
nourished
by love

I listen to
my vision

I am
Present

MY EFFORTS HELP ME

succeed

I have faith

IN MY ABILITIES

I AM ON THE RIGHT PATH

for me

I FIND GOOD IN
all things

I am open

**TO SEEING MYSELF
IN A NEW LIGHT**

I AM ALWAYS
learning

I am strong

IN MIND, BODY & SPIRIT

I give myself

ROOM TO GROW

I am in charge

OF MY OWN

HAPPINESS

I EMBRACE

who I am

I LET GO OF PAST BELIEFS THAT

no longer serve me

MY POWER
IS ON THE
INSIDE

MY IMPERFECTIONS ARE WHAT MAKE ME
unique

My needs matter

I acknowledge

MY OWN SELF-WORTH

I AM WORTHY OF
celebrating myself

I EVOLVE
everyday

My feelings

DESERVE TO BE EXPRESSED

OF WHO I AM
BECOMING

I SET MY
boundaries

Asking for help

IS A GIFT I GIVE MYSELF AND OTHERS

THE ONLY
APPROVAL I NEED

is my own

I trust
WHAT IS WITHIN ME

I ALLOW MYSELF TO HEAL

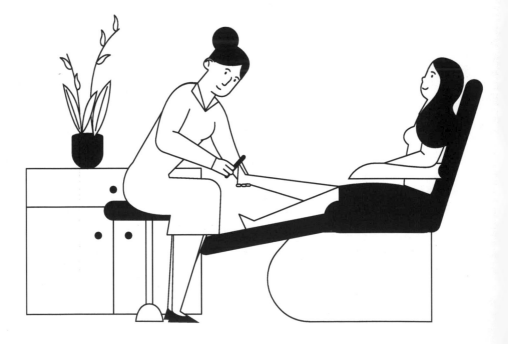

I REST
when my body & mind
TELL ME TO

i live in love

66
I LET GO OF
WHAT I CANNOT
CHANGE

I LIVE IN THE
MOMENT

I TREAT MY
BODY WITH
CARE AND
LOVE

I was born to
love
and be loved

I AM

Exactly Who I need To Be

I am

Made in the USA
Las Vegas, NV
08 January 2022

40827402R00062